© 2011 By Deborah Leoni

Published by That's Life Inspirations
by arrangement with the author.
All rights reserved. No part of this publication may be reproduced,
Stored in a retrieval system, or transmitted in any form by any means,
electronic, mechanical, photocopying, recording or otherwise,
without prior written permission from the author.
2nd Edition
ISBN: 978-0-9850615-1-7
Printed and bound in the United States of America

www.thatslifeinspirations.com

## A Widows Book of Prayer and Life Journal

- Introduction....................................................................................................P.3

- Seven Prayers for the Seven Days of the Week.................................P.7

- Prayer to Surrender Grief to God...........................................................P.21

- Prayer to Find Meaning in the Meaningless......................................P.23

- Prayer for the Ability to Learn New Tasks..........................................P.25

- Prayer for Patience ....................................................................................P.27

- Prayer for Strength....................................................................................P.29

- Prayer for Decision That Need to be Made.......................................P.31

- Prayer for My Encounters with Friends and Family.......................P.33

- Prayer for Uncomfortable Situations...................................................P.35

- Prayer for Physical and Emotional well being..................................P.37

- Prayer for all the 1sts as you Traverse the Territory alone that would have been Shared with your Partner..............................................P.39

- Prayer for the Precious Memories........................................................P.41

- Journaling Pages.........................................................................................P.42

- In Closing; A Personal Story....................................................................P.57

# Introduction

First and foremost I want to express my condolences to you and your family. If you have purchased this prayer book, at some point you have lost a loved one. I have written this book as a result of losing someone very close to me. By writing this book I thought I could help other people who were also going through the grief process and possibly help bring them closer to God.

I would like to give you a little bit of instruction on how to go about using this book. My intention was for you to be able to carry this book with you anywhere that you may go. I wanted it to be easy to access and available any time you felt you needed some strength, comfort or encouragement.

In the beginning words are very hard to come by. It's hard to explain to family and friends what has happened. It's hard to speak to God. The only way to begin the grief process is to pray and seek solace. I found that trying to come up with the words that I was looking for was just impossible. My mind was always blank, always off in another direction. I could not focus. I could not concentrate on what I was trying to do. There were many times I would even just sit and stare out the back door or just look at the wall. The TV was running constantly, but I did not retain anything. At that point the most important thing to me was to try to express myself.

I would look to God for answers, but I couldn't seem to compose a simple sentence. I couldn't get a question out, I couldn't even think correctly. It took a lot of time just to come around and understand what I wanted to say. I was angry with God. I was frustrated. My family was trying to say things to make me feel better. None of it was relevant. Finally I had to sit down with pen and paper and compose some prayers that I could actually read without thinking about it too hard. This helped me focus a great deal.

That was when I decided to use all of my feelings, all of my experiences and all of my basic emotions to try to help someone else get through the process that I was going through. I thought back to the most difficult times and started there.

In the first section you will find prayers for everyday; Sunday through Saturday. They represent the first week after someone has died. That is the week that you are trying to make funeral arrangements, explain to family and friends what's happened and try to come to terms with what's going on.

Ask people to help you. I know you're not used to people helping you. It's all very difficult. You may need to use this section for the first couple of weeks, maybe even the first month. You may not be prepared or ready for the remaining sections. Take your time, there is no rush. The grief process is a slow, steady process. Each person will progress at a different rate.

In the second section you will find various prayers for various activities and feelings that you need help with. Things don't always happen the way we anticipate they should. A lot of things take us by surprise. The person that you have lost may have done certain things around the house or performed certain daily tasks that you have either, never had to do, or done very infrequently. This is the section that you can scroll through and look and see which prayer is appropriate for your current immediate need.

Make no mistake; this book is not a book about the grief process. It explains nothing about why you feel the way you do. Nor does it define the steps or phases of grief. What it does is give you a voice. It provides the words to use in a prayer when words are failing us. There are no words to explain how we feel. There are prayers we can use to once again be close to our Lord to break the ice and begin speaking to him again whether for the first time or to reconcile with him.

Often in grief we blame God for the death. So it is sometimes hard to talk with him. We do not trust him fully after such a tremendous loss. We are angry, disappointed and frustrated. At times like this words can simply refuse to come.

In this book of prayer are the words you can use until you are once again able to find your own voice and your relationship with God has been reconciled. We must always trust God and know that his ways are higher than our ways and that he knows what is best for us. We don't see it at the time but we must trust that this is the case.

On each page I have included a Scripture. The Scriptures will be helpful to you. You may not have your Bible with you constantly to look up the Scripture and to read the exact context, so I have provided you the basic Scripture to support the prayer that you were saying. Once you feel more comfortable speaking with God, then reading his word will also become easier. I have also included a journaling section in the book for you to record your own thoughts. You may want to write your own prayers. Sometimes just writing what you feel will bring it out in the open and you can see your needs.

My goal in writing this book and preparing it in the format that I have was to help, comfort and ease the passage of time. Very often time seems to drag, or rush by so fast it's impossible to keep up with. Your sense of time may be skewed. There may come a time when you simply wake up and feel like you have missed a large section of your life. It is my hope that during this time you can use this prayer book to enhance your experience with the Lord and gain comfort to get through every day. A special prayer for you follows:

>My prayer for you today is that you will love yourself as your spouse loved you and as your friends and family love you. Most of all that you will know that God loves you and wants to see you prosper and be happy. He has made provision for us so that we can achieve just that.
>
>Grab hold of all God has to offer you and never let go. Stay in his will and your joy will truly be full. You must ask him and then receive it with a joyous heart. Lift your heart to God and raise your face to the light of the world.

Pray Without Ceasing,
Deborah A. Leoni

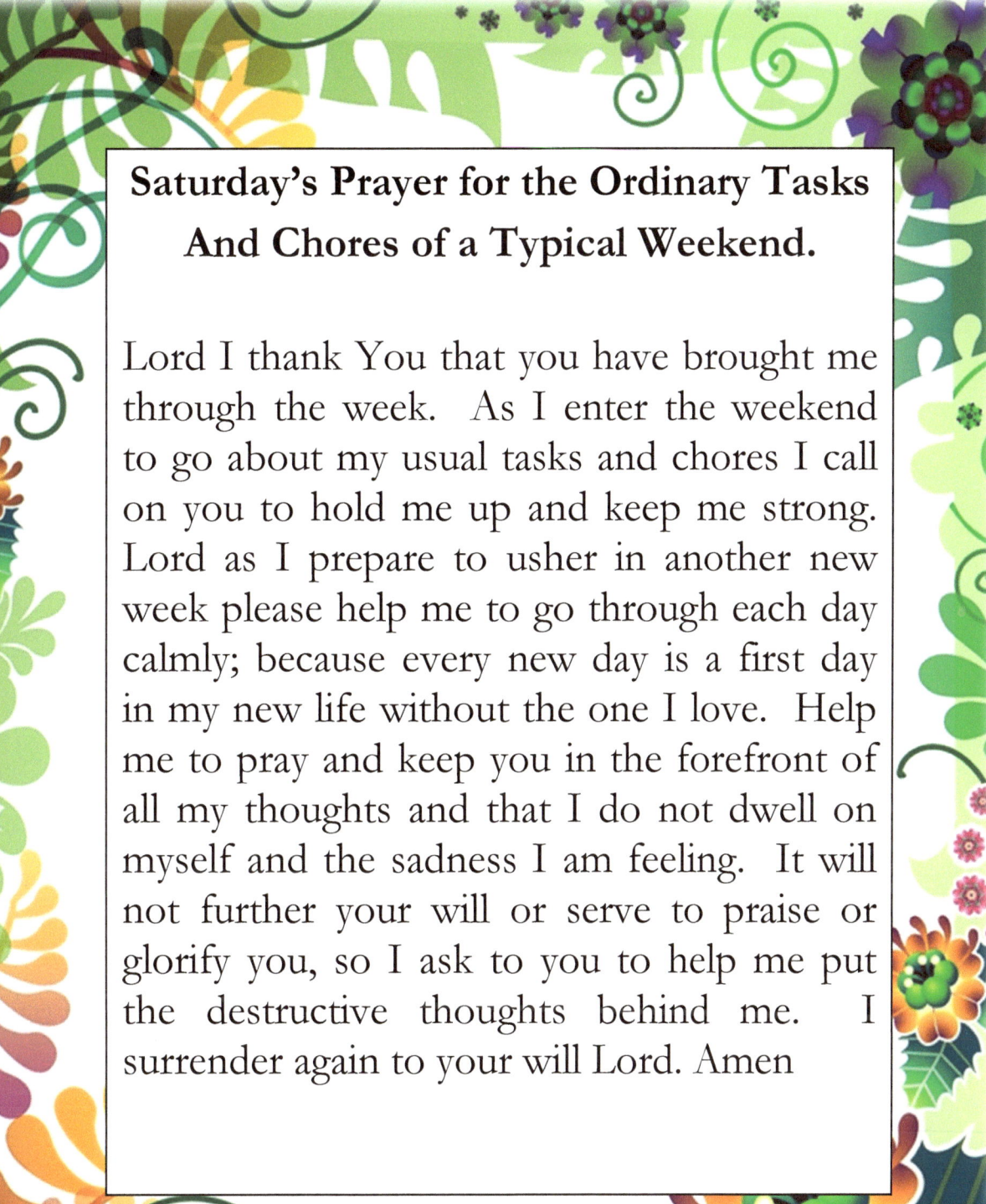

**Saturday's Prayer for the Ordinary Tasks And Chores of a Typical Weekend.**

Lord I thank You that you have brought me through the week. As I enter the weekend to go about my usual tasks and chores I call on you to hold me up and keep me strong. Lord as I prepare to usher in another new week please help me to go through each day calmly; because every new day is a first day in my new life without the one I love. Help me to pray and keep you in the forefront of all my thoughts and that I do not dwell on myself and the sadness I am feeling. It will not further your will or serve to praise or glorify you, so I ask to you to help me put the destructive thoughts behind me. I surrender again to your will Lord. Amen

## Psalm 34:17-18

**(New International Version)**

**17** The righteous cry out, and the LORD hears them; he delivers them from all their troubles.

**18** The LORD is close to the brokenhearted and saves those who are crushed in spirit.

## Luke 12; 29-31

**(New International Version)**

**29** And do not set your heart on what you will eat or drink; do not worry about it.

**30** For the pagan world runs after all such things, and your Father knows that you need them.

**31** But seek his kingdom, and these things will be given to you as well.

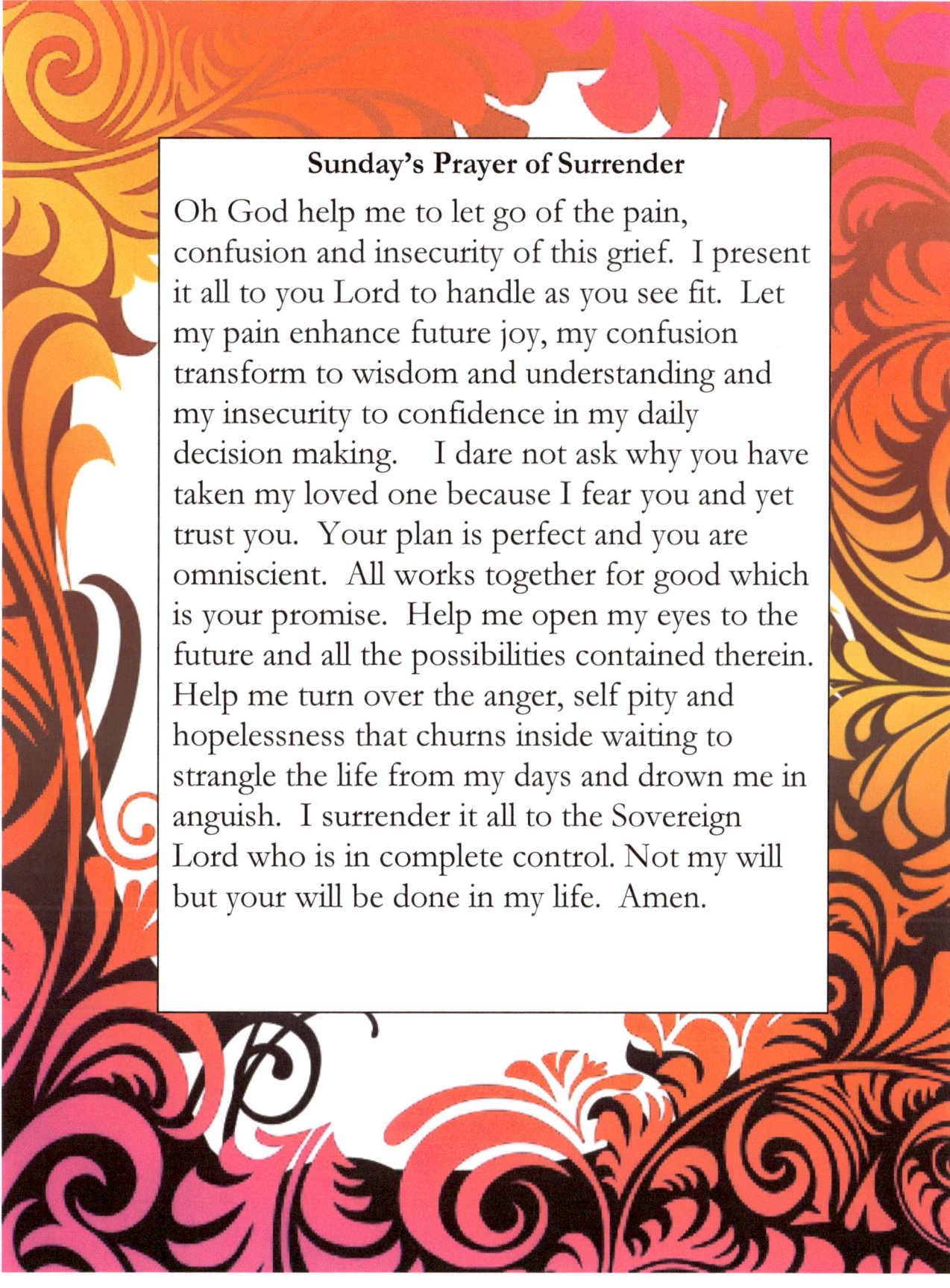

### Sunday's Prayer of Surrender

Oh God help me to let go of the pain, confusion and insecurity of this grief. I present it all to you Lord to handle as you see fit. Let my pain enhance future joy, my confusion transform to wisdom and understanding and my insecurity to confidence in my daily decision making. I dare not ask why you have taken my loved one because I fear you and yet trust you. Your plan is perfect and you are omniscient. All works together for good which is your promise. Help me open my eyes to the future and all the possibilities contained therein. Help me turn over the anger, self pity and hopelessness that churns inside waiting to strangle the life from my days and drown me in anguish. I surrender it all to the Sovereign Lord who is in complete control. Not my will but your will be done in my life. Amen.

## 1 Peter 5:7

**(New International Version)**

**7** Cast all your anxiety on him because he cares for you.

## 2 Corinthians 10:5

**(New International Version)**

**5** We are destroying speculations and every lofty thing raised up against the knowledge of God, and we are taking every thought captive to the obedience of Christ.

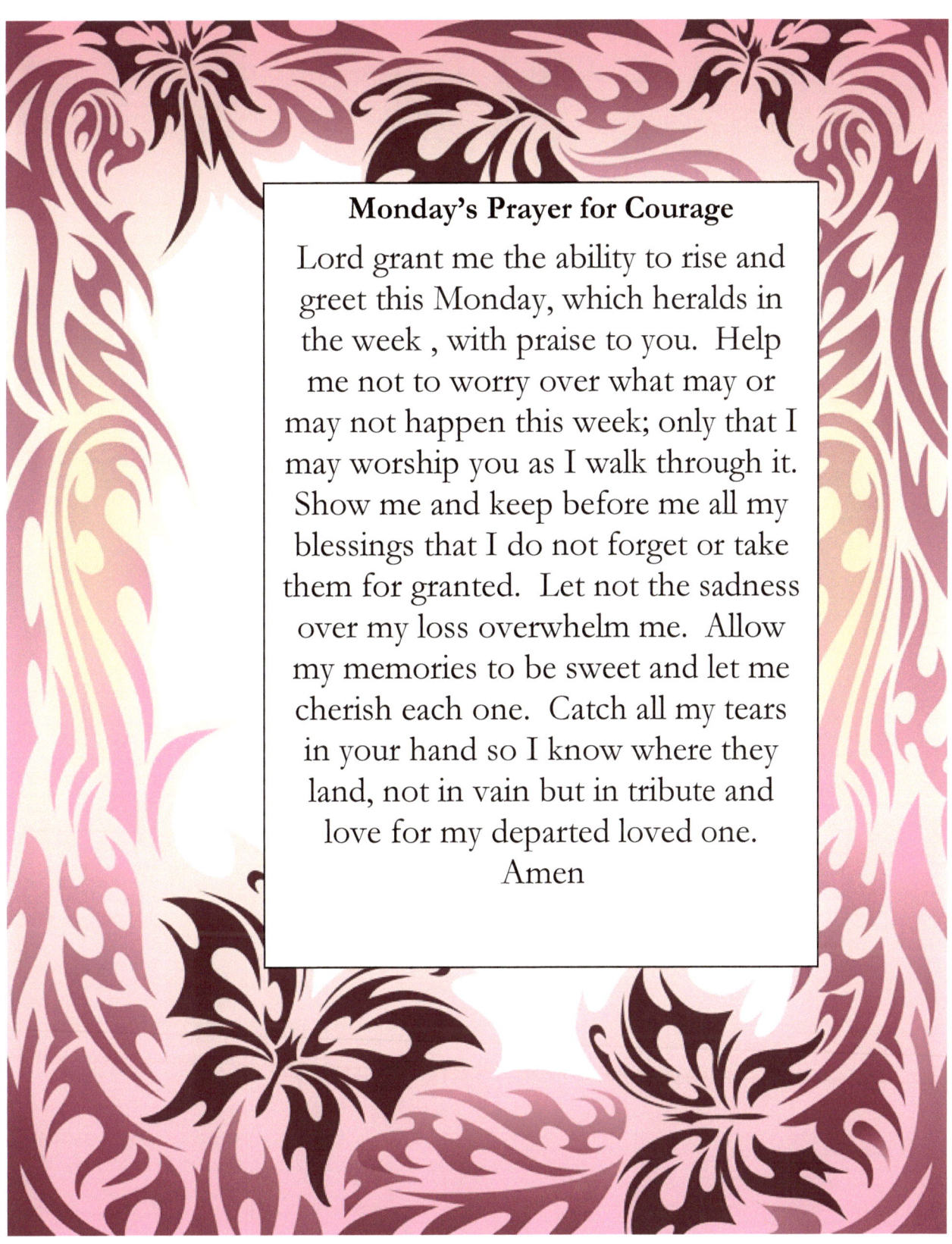

### Monday's Prayer for Courage

Lord grant me the ability to rise and greet this Monday, which heralds in the week, with praise to you. Help me not to worry over what may or may not happen this week; only that I may worship you as I walk through it. Show me and keep before me all my blessings that I do not forget or take them for granted. Let not the sadness over my loss overwhelm me. Allow my memories to be sweet and let me cherish each one. Catch all my tears in your hand so I know where they land, not in vain but in tribute and love for my departed loved one.
Amen

## Proverbs 3:5-6

### (New International Version)

**5** Trust in the LORD with all your heart
   and lean not on your own understanding;
**6** in all your ways submit to him,
   and he will make your paths straight.

## Matthew 6:6

### (King James Version)

**6** But thou, when thou prayest, enter into thy closet, and when thou hast shut thy door, pray to thy Father which is in secret; and thy Father which seeth in secret shall reward thee openly.

## Tuesday's Prayer to Find
## A Reason to go on.

Lord show me why I alone remain. Show me what your plan is for my life now that half of my world is gone and forever altered. The half that remains seems to have no real purpose, no motivation no reason to be. Show me your perfect and unalterable plan Lord. I cannot see for the tears. I cannot fathom your goal. Where is the life lesson in this and how can it glorify you? Lord enter into that empty place. Show me the next steps to take; but please be gentle as I am fragile.   Amen

# Matthew 6:9-13

## (King James Version)

**9** After this manner therefore pray ye: Our Father which art in heaven, Hallowed be thy name.

**10** Thy kingdom come, Thy will be done in earth, as it is in heaven.

**11** Give us this day our daily bread,

**12** And forgive us our debts, as we forgive our debtors.

**13** And lead us not into temptation, but deliver us from evil: For thine is the kingdom, and the power, and the glory, for ever. Amen.

## Wednesday's Prayer for Focus

Lord I seek your direction to keep me focused on the most important tasks. I ask for your guidance as I prioritize for the day and the remainder of the week. Help me focus on the things that will be the most important and not get caught up in the mundane and irrelevant. The list is long Lord and I seek your perfect order of importance. Amen

# Lamentations 3:22-25

## (New International Version)

**22** Because of the LORD's great love we are not consumed, for his compassions never fail.
**23** They are new every morning; great is your faithfulness.
**24** I say to myself, "The LORD is my portion; therefore I will wait for Him."

**25** The LORD is good to those whose hope is in Him, to the one who seeks Him.

## Thursday's Prayer to Release What Never Belonged to Me.

Thank You Lord for all the Blessings and gifts you have bestowed upon me. Thank you for the time I was given with my beloved husband. You gave him to me for a time to love, honor and cherish. I will not shake my fist at you, blame you, or be disrespectful of you for that will accomplish nothing. You have called my loved one home and that is all I need to know. Help me Lord to release my loved one to you as he does indeed belong to you, as you are his creator. You knew when he was created the number of his days. Your plan is perfect, the length of time you allowed us to spend together just the right amount to accomplish your goal in the shaping of each of us. I release him to you Lord as he never belonged to me; but I know we will be together again in eternity and walk with you. That is enough for me to know right now. Praise to you Lord, you are good, you are in control and you are the Almighty. Amen

# Matthew 5:6

(New International Version)

**6** Blessed are those who hunger and thirst for righteousness, for they will be filled.

# Ephesians 5:17-18

(New International Version)

**17** So then do not be foolish, but understand what the will of the Lord is.

**18** And do not get drunk with wine, for that is dissipation, but be filled with the Spirit.

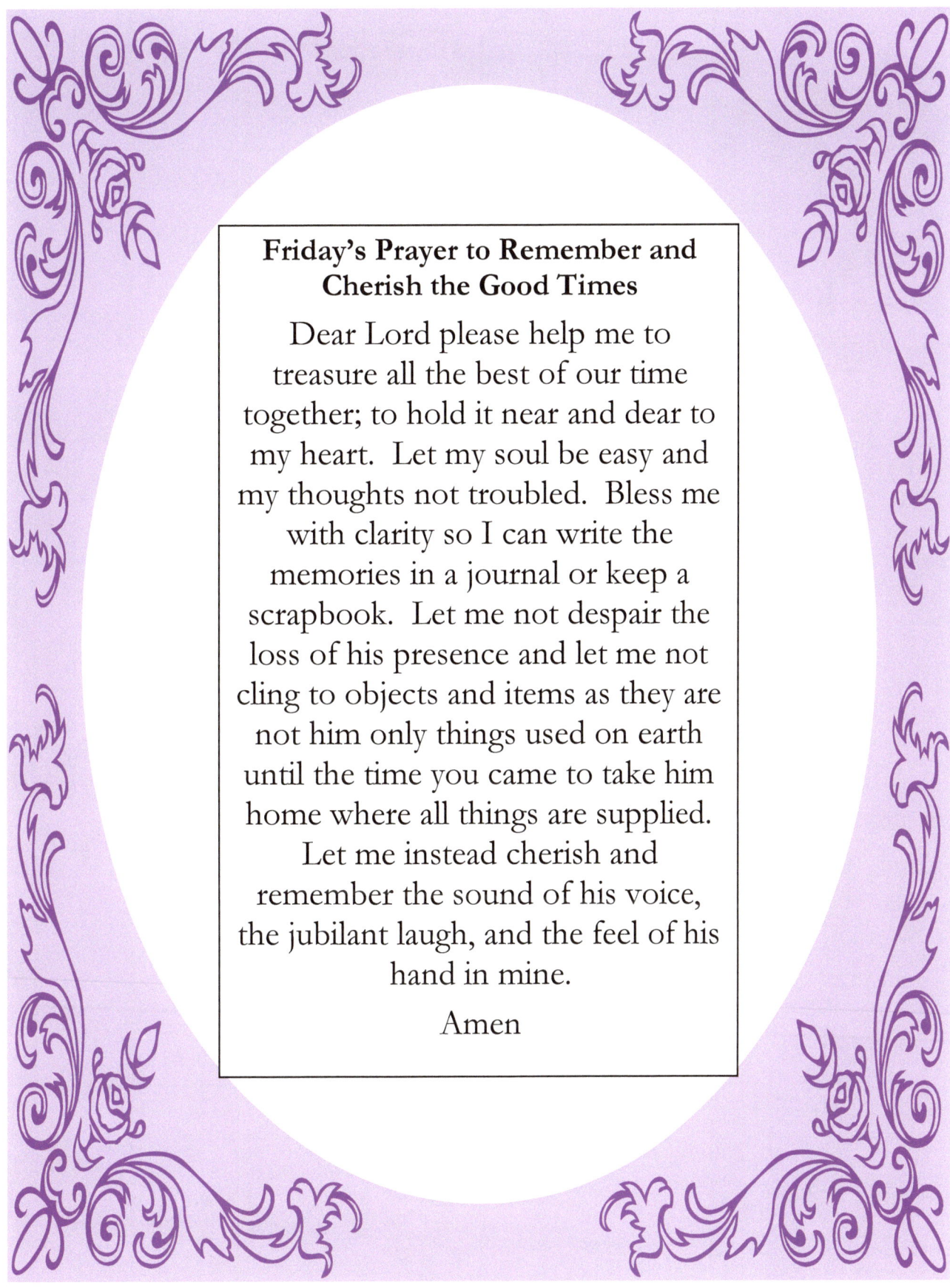

**Friday's Prayer to Remember and Cherish the Good Times**

Dear Lord please help me to treasure all the best of our time together; to hold it near and dear to my heart. Let my soul be easy and my thoughts not troubled. Bless me with clarity so I can write the memories in a journal or keep a scrapbook. Let me not despair the loss of his presence and let me not cling to objects and items as they are not him only things used on earth until the time you came to take him home where all things are supplied. Let me instead cherish and remember the sound of his voice, the jubilant laugh, and the feel of his hand in mine.

Amen

## Romans 8:26

### (New International Version)

**26** In the same way, the Spirit helps us in our weakness. We do not know what we ought to pray for, but the Spirit himself intercedes for us through wordless groans.

## I Timothy 2:1

### (New International Version)

**1** First of all, I urge that entreaties and prayers, petitions and thanksgivings, be made on behalf of all men.

**Prayer to Surrender Grief to God**

Our Father who art in Heaven Hallowed be they name. Thy Kingdom come, thy will be done on earth as it is in Heaven. Your will has been done. My grief is all consuming. I allow this grief to pour forth and I surrender it to you Lord.

I rest myself in your comforting arms and as I do my sorrow flows to you. You absorb all I have and are my comfort and my help.

I thank you Lord for taking all this from me and I seek your face as I struggle to understand that which is beyond me. Amen

## 1 Timothy 5:5

**(New International Version)**

**5** The widow who is really in need and left all alone puts her hope in God and continues night and day to pray and to ask God for help.

## Luke 12:7

**(New International Version)**

7 Indeed, the very hairs of your head are all numbered. Don't be afraid; you are worth more than many sparrows.

## Prayer to Find Meaning in the Meaningless

Lord I ask you to grant me understanding and wisdom to deal with this great loss. My thoughts and ways cannot compare to your great wisdom; but I trust you to guide me and show me what you feel I can comprehend. In all things I will seek your face and everything else will follow. The wisdom, knowledge and understanding I seek is there for the asking. I thank you for the journey even though the why of it is lost to me just now. I realize all experiences, great or small are events of refinement intended for our growth. They are used by you Lord to mold and teach us, just as Joseph understood that his treatment by his brothers was meant to do him harm but was used by you for good. Amen

## Luke 11:9-10

**(New International Version)**

**9** "So I say to you: Ask and it will be given to you; seek and you will find; knock and the door will be opened to you.

**10** For everyone who asks receives; the one who seeks finds; and to the one who knocks, the door will be opened.

## Ecclesiastes 9:7
**(New International Version)**

**7** Go, eat your food with gladness, and drink your wine with a joyful heart, for God has already approved what you do.

## Prayer for the Ability To Learn New Tasks

Lord I ask you to help me in my daily routine to keep my mind sharp and alert; to help me ask for help and instruction when needed without feeling embarrassed or ignorant. As I tackle the chores my spouse handled effortlessly and happily let me do so also. Let the doing of it somehow honor my loved one and help me relish the challenge of it. Thank you Lord for the ability to do all things through your strength. Amen

## Luke 12:27,28

**(New International Version)**

**27** "Consider how the wild flowers grow. They do not labor or spin. Yet I tell you, not even Solomon in all his splendor was dressed like one of these.

**28** If that is how God clothes the grass of the field, which is here today, and tomorrow is thrown into the fire, how much more will he clothe you—you of little faith!

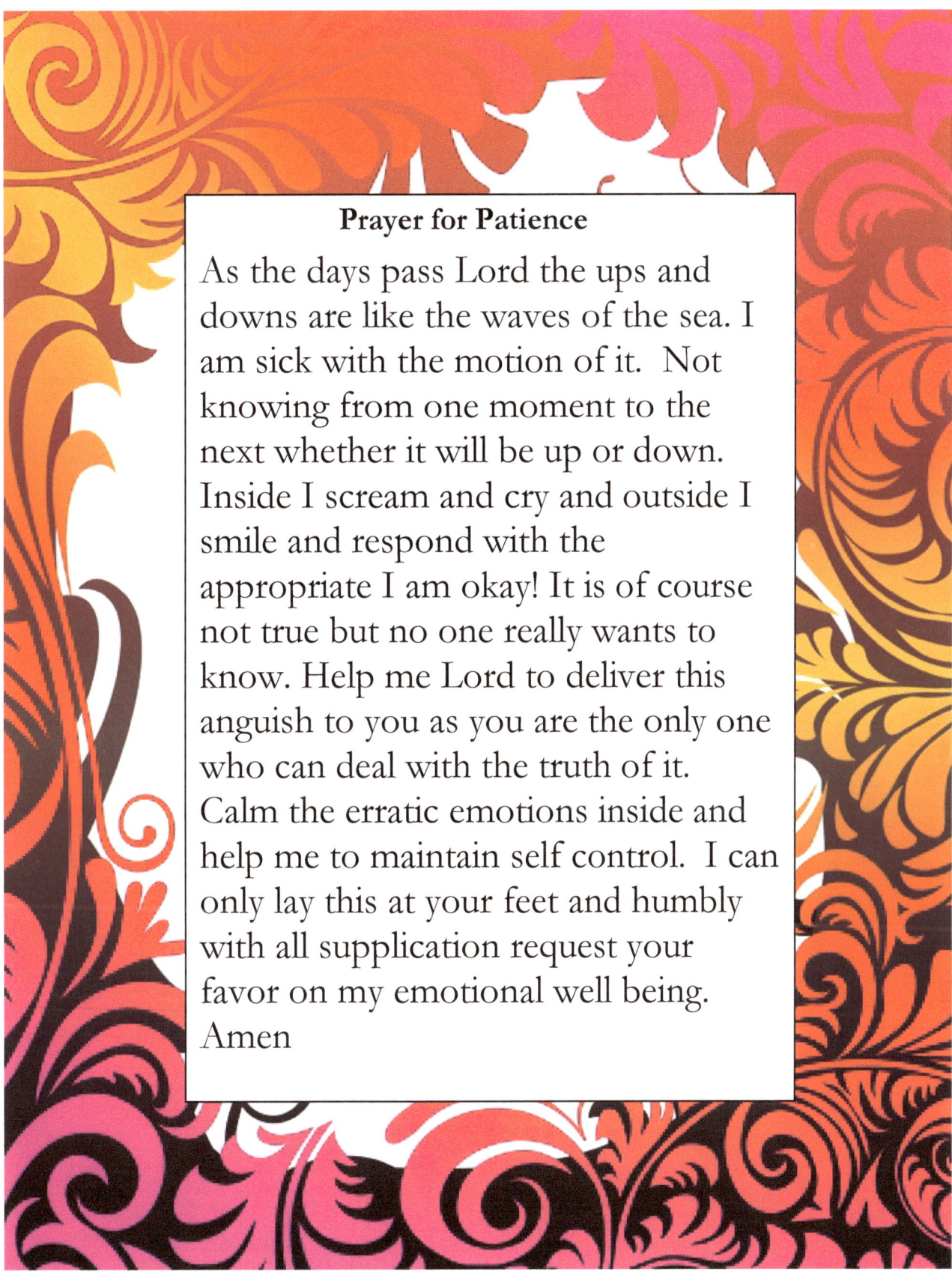

### Prayer for Patience

As the days pass Lord the ups and downs are like the waves of the sea. I am sick with the motion of it. Not knowing from one moment to the next whether it will be up or down. Inside I scream and cry and outside I smile and respond with the appropriate I am okay! It is of course not true but no one really wants to know. Help me Lord to deliver this anguish to you as you are the only one who can deal with the truth of it. Calm the erratic emotions inside and help me to maintain self control. I can only lay this at your feet and humbly with all supplication request your favor on my emotional well being. Amen

## Ecclesiastes 3:1-4
### (King James Version)

**1** To everything there is a season, and a time to every purpose under the heaven:

**2** A time to be born, and a time to die; a time to plant, and a time to pluck up that which is planted;

**3** A time to kill, and a time to heal; a time to break down, and a time to build up;

**4** A time to weep, and a time to laugh; a time to mourn, and a time to dance;

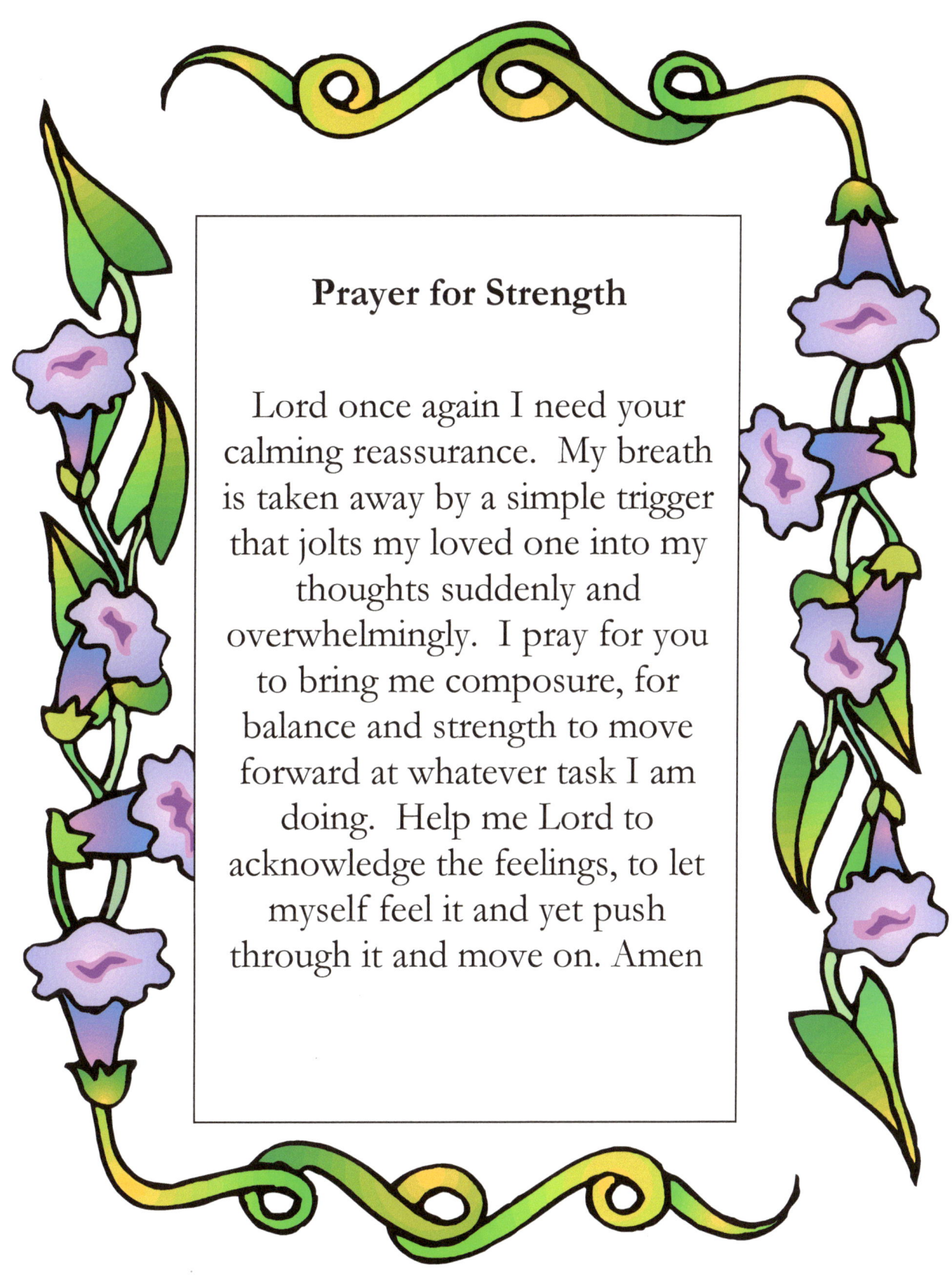

## Prayer for Strength

Lord once again I need your calming reassurance. My breath is taken away by a simple trigger that jolts my loved one into my thoughts suddenly and overwhelmingly. I pray for you to bring me composure, for balance and strength to move forward at whatever task I am doing. Help me Lord to acknowledge the feelings, to let myself feel it and yet push through it and move on. Amen

## Philippians 4:6-7

### (New International Version)

**6** Do not be anxious about anything, but in every situation, by prayer and petition, with thanksgiving, present your requests to God.

**7** And the peace of God, which transcends all understanding, will guard your hearts and your minds in Christ Jesus.

**Prayer for Decisions
That Need to be Made**

Lord I bring to you my questions, fears and options. You are my constant help as I traverse the path alone. Guide my thoughts and keep me on the path which you have selected for me. I thank you Lord for your plan for me and I seek your will in my life. I ask you to point me in the right direction. All my thoughts I give to you to shape, form and train up. I bring all my choices to you for your approval and guidance as I make those hard decisions Lord. Amen

## Matthew 11:28-30

**(New International Version)**

**28** "Come to me, all you who are weary and burdened, and I will give you rest.

**29** Take my yoke upon you and learn from me, for I am gentle and humble in heart, and you will find rest for your souls.

**30** For my yoke is easy and my burden is light."

**Prayer for My Encounters with Family and Friends**

Lord I come to you today for tolerance, understanding and courage; not only for me, but for all my friends and family. We are all dealing with this event in different ways. Please allow us the concern and consideration to tolerate each other's responses and actions to this trying time in all of our lives. Lord give us the desire to learn from each other and help to understand each other. Lord help us to show each other the love we have for one another and the ability to exercise patience for our differences in the way we show grief. I thank you Lord, for your assistance and grace, as we go through each day.
Amen

## 2 Corinthians 5:17
### (King James Version)

**17**Therefore if any man be in Christ, he is a new creature: old things are passed away; behold, all things are become new.

## Job 34:10
### (New International Version)

**10**"So listen to me, you men of understanding.
 Far be it from God to do evil,
 from the Almighty to do wrong.

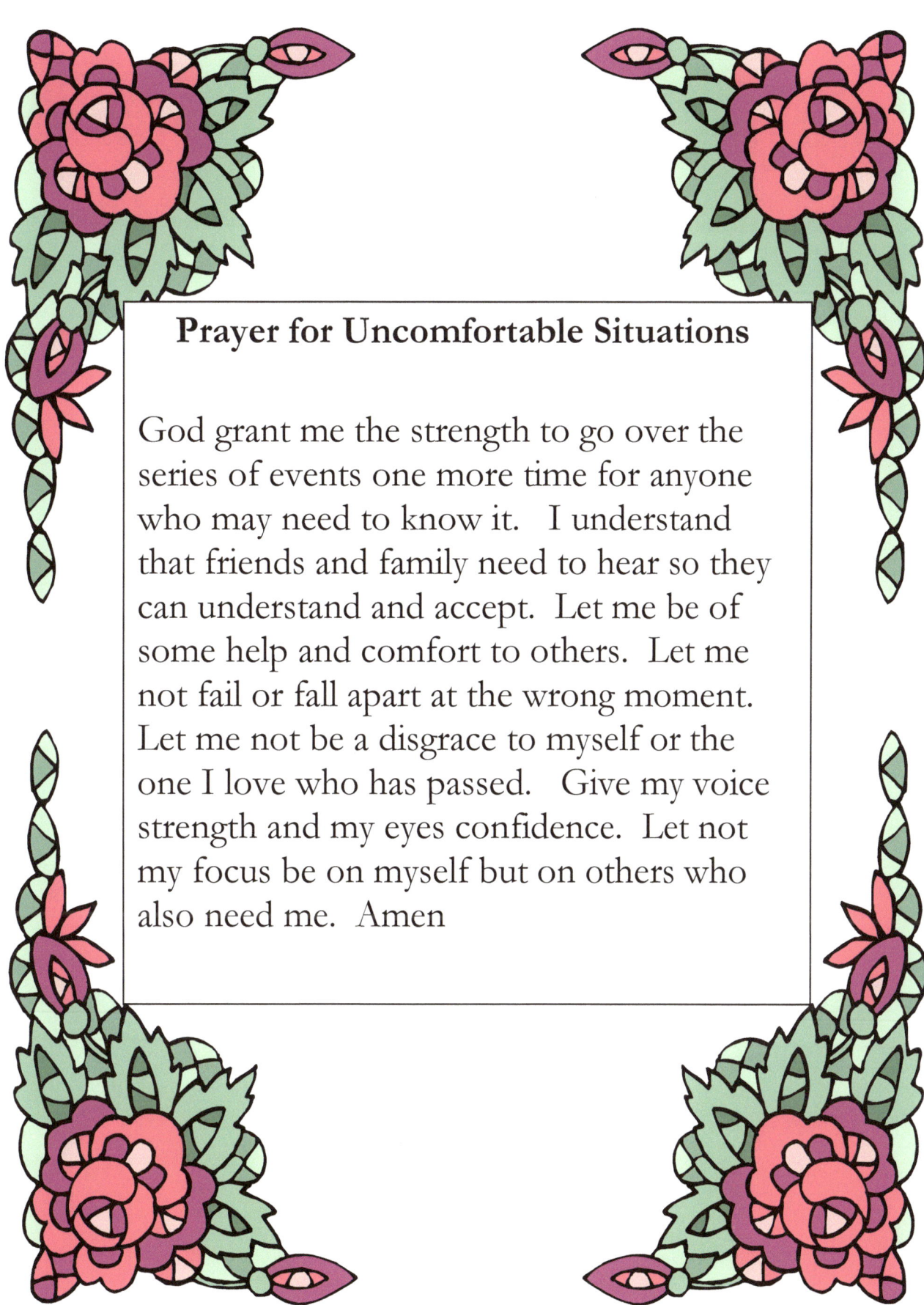

## Prayer for Uncomfortable Situations

God grant me the strength to go over the series of events one more time for anyone who may need to know it. I understand that friends and family need to hear so they can understand and accept. Let me be of some help and comfort to others. Let me not fail or fall apart at the wrong moment. Let me not be a disgrace to myself or the one I love who has passed. Give my voice strength and my eyes confidence. Let not my focus be on myself but on others who also need me. Amen

## John 14:27

### (New International Version)

**27** Peace I leave with you; my peace I give you. I do not give to you as the world gives. Do not let your hearts be troubled and do not be afraid.

## 2 Corinthians 5:1

### (New International Version)

**1** For we know that if the earthly tent we live in is destroyed, we have a building from God, an eternal house in heaven, not built by human hands.

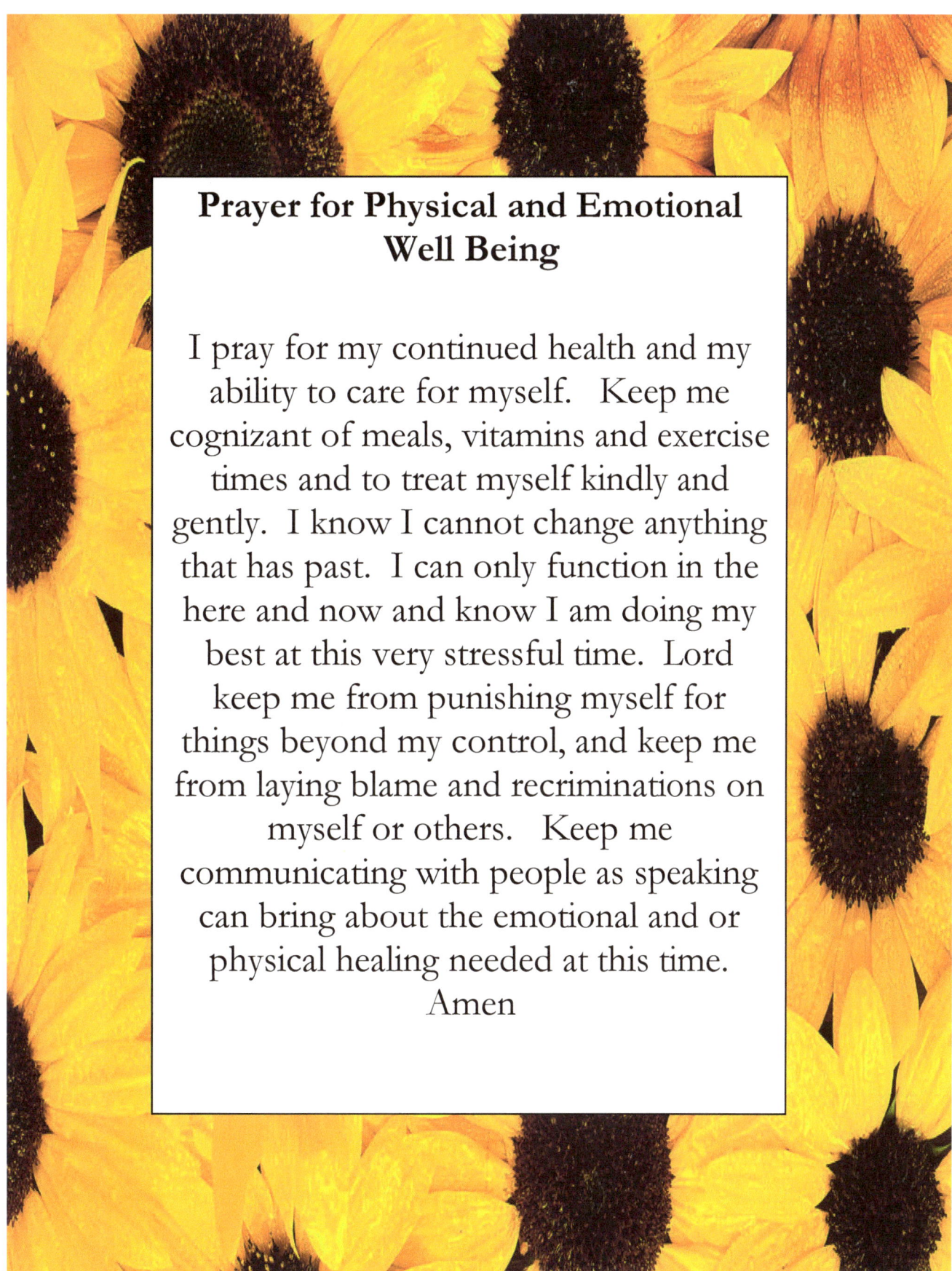

## Prayer for Physical and Emotional Well Being

I pray for my continued health and my ability to care for myself.  Keep me cognizant of meals, vitamins and exercise times and to treat myself kindly and gently.  I know I cannot change anything that has past.  I can only function in the here and now and know I am doing my best at this very stressful time.  Lord keep me from punishing myself for things beyond my control, and keep me from laying blame and recriminations on myself or others.  Keep me communicating with people as speaking can bring about the emotional and or physical healing needed at this time.
Amen

# Jeremiah 29:11-13

## (New International Version)

**11** For I know the plans I have for you," declares the LORD, "plans to prosper you and not to harm you, plans to give you hope and a future.

**12** Then you will call on me and come and pray to me, and I will listen to you.

**13** You will seek me and find me when you seek me with all your heart.

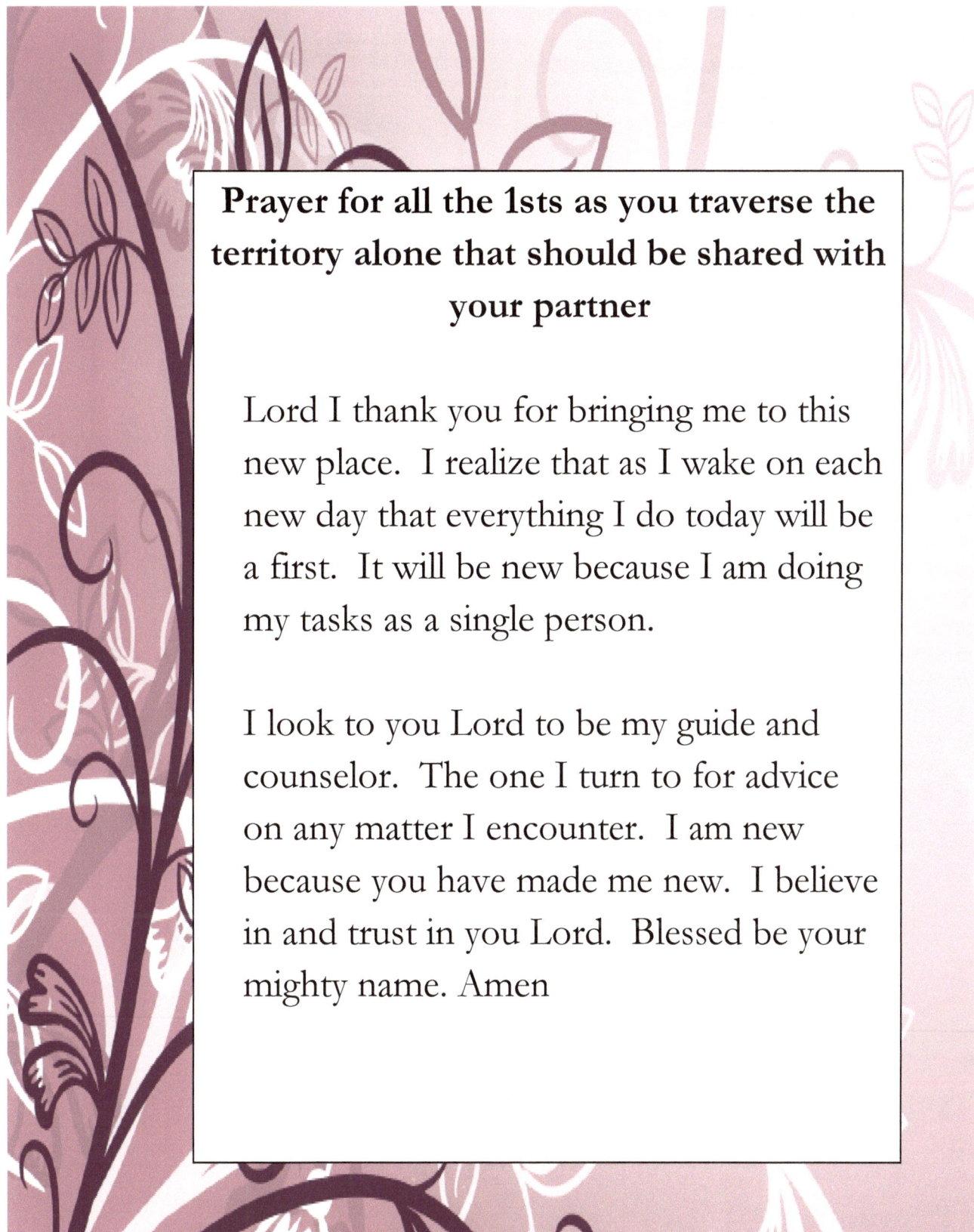

**Prayer for all the 1sts as you traverse the territory alone that should be shared with your partner**

Lord I thank you for bringing me to this new place. I realize that as I wake on each new day that everything I do today will be a first. It will be new because I am doing my tasks as a single person.

I look to you Lord to be my guide and counselor. The one I turn to for advice on any matter I encounter. I am new because you have made me new. I believe in and trust in you Lord. Blessed be your mighty name. Amen

## Psalm 43:5

### (New International Version)

**5** Why, my soul, are you downcast?
   Why so disturbed within me?  Put your hope in God, for I will yet praise him,
   my Savior and my God.

## Psalm 51:1

### (King James Version)

**1** Have mercy upon me, O God, according to thy loving kindness: according unto the multitude of thy tender mercies blot out my transgressions.

## Prayer for the Precious Memories.

Lord each memory of my loved one is precious to me and I thank you for the time you gave to us. I ask you to guard my mind and heart and let the wonderful memories reside there. That I may revisit those times with joy and gladness knowing that, by your grace, I will see my loved one again. Keep them fresh and clear and not faded and distorted so my joy can be renewed. In your glorious name be the power. Amen

Journaling Pages

## In Closing
## A Personal Story

I held my wedding dress in my hands today. I caressed the satin and touched the lace to my cheek. I remembered the best day of my life. The joy, the laughter, the emotions and the all the friends and family, who were there to wish us well, came flooding back to my mind.

My husband has been gone two years, six months and 13 days. Yes, I still count the days and yes it still is very painful and I cry sometimes. The good news is that now I can smile, laugh and enjoy the memories that shaped my life and made me who I am.

I thank God every day for the time I was given with my husband. I would not trade it for anything. I am a better person for having shared my life with him and I know he would want me to go on and do as many wonderful things as I could and to be as happy as I can.

I can still hear his laugh, his cautions, and his advice and feel his hugs. May that blessing never leave me. He was a doer, a guy who loved life and tried new things. He loved his friends and family and wanted the best for everyone. It is time now for me to carry on that legacy.

It is time for me to get back into the world of the living and be a doer. I thank God for my health and my ability to do just that. I ask Him also, what does He want me to do first? Where can I help and be of service to Him. He tells me I have just completed my first task in writing this prayer book.

I am delighted to serve the Lord, come to terms with my loss and help someone else in the same position as I was. I pray this book helps you through your desert and to climb your mountain as much as it helped me while writing it.

To submit a prayer request or contact me please go to thatslifeinspirations.com and click on the Prayer request button on any page. I look forward to hearing from you with any feedback you may have.

May God bless you and keep you in his perfect peace. Amen

www.ingramcontent.com/pod-product-compliance
Lightning Source LLC
Chambersburg PA
CBHW040056160426
43192CB00002B/80